Collins

KS1
Maths & English
10 Minute Tests

Brad Thompson and Jon Goulding

How to Use this Book

This book consists of maths and English tests for children in Key Stage 1. Each test is designed to be completed in approximately 10 minutes.

This book contains:

- 8 Maths Arithmetic tests
- 8 Maths Reasoning tests
- 8 English Reading tests
- 8 English Grammar and Punctuation tests
- 8 English Spelling tests

Clearly laid out questions and easy-to-use answers will help your child to improve their understanding and gain confidence.

The tests are all the same level of difficulty, which means they can be carried out in any order and at any time throughout Year 2 to provide invaluable practice for your child.

Children should work in a quiet environment where they can complete each test undisturbed. They should complete each test in approximately 10 minutes.

The number of marks available for each question is given on the right-hand side of the test pages, with a total provided at the end of each test.

In the Reasoning tests, each test begins with one aural question. You will need to help your child by reading out the question. Instructions are given in the Answers section on page 95.

For the Spelling tests, you will need to help your child by reading out the words they are required to spell. Instructions are given in the Answers section on page 109.

Answers and marking guidance are provided for each test. A score chart can be found at the back of the book, which your child can use to record their marks and see their progress.

Acknowledgements

The authors and publisher are grateful to the copyright holders for permission to use quoted materials and images.

Images are © Shutterstock.com and © HarperCollinsPublishers

Every effort has been made to trace copyright holders and obtain their permission for the use of copyright material. The authors and publisher will gladly receive information enabling them to rectify any error or omission in subsequent editions. All facts are correct at time of going to press.

Published by Collins
An imprint of HarperCollinsPublishers
1 London Bridge Street
London SE1 9GF

HarperCollinsPublishers
Macken House, 39/40 Mayor Street Upper,
Dublin 1, D01 C9W8, Ireland

ISBN 9780008398835

© HarperCollinsPublishers Limited 2020

Content first published 2020

10 9 8 7 6 5

All rights reserved. No part of this publication may be reproduced, stored in a retrieval system, or transmitted, in any form or by any means, electronic, mechanical, photocopying, recording or otherwise, without the prior permission of Collins.

British Library Cataloguing in Publication Data.

A CIP record of this book is available from the British Library.

Authors: Brad Thompson and Jon Goulding
Associate Publisher: Fiona McGlade
Editor and Project Manager: Katie Galloway
Cover Design: Kevin Robbins and Sarah Duxbury
Inside Concept Design: Ian Wrigley
Text Design and Layout: Contentra Technologies
Production: Karen Nulty
Printed in the UK by Martins the Printers

MIX
Paper | Supporting responsible forestry
FSC™ C007454
www.fsc.org

This book is produced from independently certified FSC™ paper to ensure responsible forest management.

For more information visit:
www.harpercollins.co.uk/green

Contents

Arithmetic Test 1

1 7 − 2 = ☐

1 mark

2 6 + 13 = ☐

1 mark

3 19 − 7 = ☐

1 mark

4 33 + 33 = ☐

1 mark

5 5 × 8 = ☐

1 mark

6 18 ÷ 2 = ☐

1 mark

7 | $63 - 6 = \boxed{}$

1 mark

8 | $4 + 58 = \boxed{}$

1 mark

9 | $\boxed{} = 29 - 6$

1 mark

10 | $\dfrac{1}{4}$ of $8 = \boxed{}$

1 mark

11 | $\dfrac{1}{2}$ of $70 = \boxed{}$

1 mark

12 | $85 - 18 = \boxed{}$

1 mark

Test 1 total marks ..../12

5

10 min

1 $4 + 13 + 2 = \boxed{}$

1 mark

2 $19 - 6 = \boxed{}$

1 mark

3 $50 - 20 = \boxed{}$

1 mark

4 $12 \times 10 = \boxed{}$

1 mark

5 $95 + 9 = \boxed{}$

1 mark

6 $\boxed{} + 8 = 33$

1 mark

7   50 ÷ 10 = ☐

1 mark

8   45 + 40 = ☐

1 mark

9 $\frac{1}{4}$ of 12 = ☐

1 mark

10   57 − 30 = ☐

1 mark

11 $\frac{2}{4}$ of 44 = ☐

1 mark

12   65 − 29 = ☐

1 mark

1   8 − 4 = ☐

1 mark

2   3 + 15 = ☐

1 mark

3   44 + 44 = ☐

1 mark

4   80 − 50 = ☐

1 mark

5   9 × 10 = ☐

1 mark

6   26 ÷ 2 = ☐

1 mark

7 [ ] + 6 = 24

1 mark

8 $\frac{1}{4}$ of 16 = [ ]

1 mark

9 6 + 35 = [ ]

1 mark

10 $\frac{2}{4}$ of 28 = [ ]

1 mark

11 100 − [ ] = 38

1 mark

12 46 + 39 = [ ]

1 mark

Test 3 total marks ..../12

10 min

1 14 + 5 + 1 = ☐

1 mark

2 60 − 50 = ☐

1 mark

3 18 − 6 = ☐

1 mark

4 9 × 5 = ☐

1 mark

5 59 − 32 = ☐

1 mark

6 16 ÷ 2 = ☐

1 mark

7 59 − 30 = ☐

1 mark

8 ☐ − 15 = 8

1 mark

9 8 + 59 = ☐

1 mark

10 $\frac{1}{4}$ of 20 = ☐

1 mark

11 44 + 46 = ☐

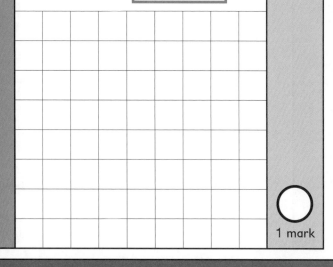

1 mark

12 $\frac{1}{2}$ of 50 = ☐

1 mark

10 min

1   18 − 6 = ☐

1 mark

2   93 + 9 = ☐

1 mark

3   24 − 11 = ☐

1 mark

4   6 × 5 = ☐

1 mark

5   66 + 22 = ☐

1 mark

6   ☐ + 8 = 32

1 mark

7 110 ÷ 10 = [ ]

1 mark

8 27 + 53 = [ ]

1 mark

9 $\frac{1}{2}$ of 80 = [ ]

1 mark

10 75 − 69 = [ ]

1 mark

11 $\frac{2}{4}$ of 20 = [ ]

1 mark

12 86 − 29 = [ ]

1 mark

Test 5 total marks ..../12

10 min

1 6 + 6 + 8 = [ ]

1 mark

2 50 − 20 = [ ]

1 mark

3 6 + 41 = [ ]

1 mark

4 98 + 9 = [ ]

1 mark

5 8 × 10 = [ ]

1 mark

6 70 ÷ 10 = [ ]

1 mark

7 57 + 40 = ⬜

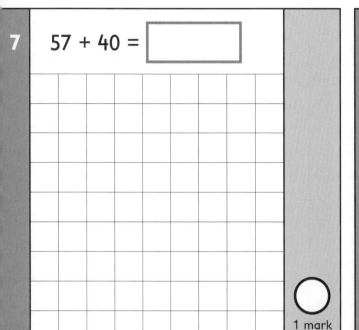

1 mark

8 67 − 9 = ⬜

1 mark

9 $\frac{1}{4}$ of 8 = ⬜

1 mark

10 $\frac{2}{4}$ of 24 = ⬜

1 mark

11 32 + 58 = ⬜

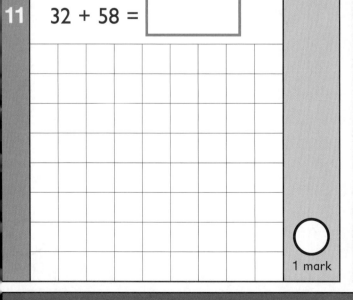

1 mark

12 100 − ⬜ = 48

1 mark

Test 6 total marks ..../12

10 min

1   8 – 6 = ☐

1 mark

2   10 + 5 + 5 = ☐

1 mark

3   80 – 30 = ☐

1 mark

4   95 + 7 = ☐

1 mark

5   11 × 5 = ☐

1 mark

6   22 ÷ 2 = ☐

1 mark

7   90 − 20 = ⬚

1 mark

8 $\frac{1}{4}$ of 28 = ⬚

1 mark

9 $\frac{1}{2}$ of 100 = ⬚

1 mark

10   ⬚ + 9 = 67

1 mark

11   ⬚ = 27 − 9

1 mark

12   76 − 69 = ⬚

1 mark

1 6 + 51 = ☐

1 mark

2 45 − 32 = ☐

1 mark

3 7 + 31 = ☐

1 mark

4 8 × 10 = ☐

1 mark

5 36 + 50 = ☐

1 mark

6 65 − 7 = ☐

1 mark

Arithmetic Test 8

7 90 ÷ 10 = ☐

1 mark

8 $\frac{1}{2}$ of 30 = ☐

1 mark

9 6 + 56 = ☐

1 mark

10 100 − ☐ = 65

1 mark

11 $\frac{2}{4}$ of 28 = ☐

1 mark

12 71 − 38 = ☐

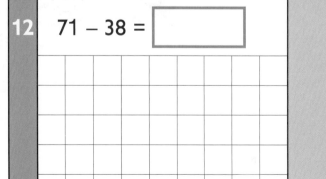

1 mark

Reasoning Tests

Jack and Sufia are children who are in some of the questions in the Reasoning tests.

There are different children mentioned in other questions as well. Their names are Mo, Grace, Leo and Meera.

Jack   **Sufia**

Mo   Grace   Leo   Meera

10 min

Aural Question

1

60 ⬜ 70

1 mark

---

2 Match each shape to the correct description.

One is done for you.

shape

| rectangle |
| triangle |
| hexagon |
| pentagon |

description

| has three vertices |
| has five equal sides |
| has four right angles |
| has six vertices |

1 mark

3 Here are two counters.

+   −

Choose a counter to make each calculation correct.

One is done for you.

5 (−) 1 = 4   25 ◯ 1 = 26

50 ◯ 1 = 51   39 ◯ 1 = 38

1 mark

4   Tick the **three** digit cards that add up to **17**

1 mark

5   Complete the number sentences.

One is done for you.

$$\frac{1}{2} \text{ of } \boxed{10} = 5$$

$$\frac{1}{2} \text{ of } \boxed{} = 6$$

1 mark

6   Match each set of satsumas to the correct multiplication.

One is done for you.

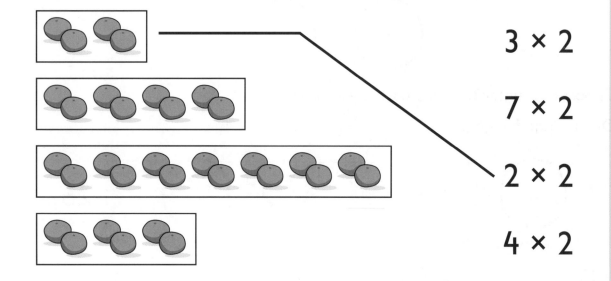

3 × 2

7 × 2

2 × 2

4 × 2

1 mark

7 Jack has 50p.

He buys an apple for **20p.**

Tick the jar that shows how much money Jack has **left.**

1 mark

8 Sufia has **40** raisins.

She shares them equally between **4** friends.

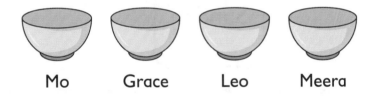

Mo   Grace   Leo   Meera

Complete the number sentence to show how Sufia shares the raisins.

$$\boxed{} \div \boxed{} = \boxed{}$$

1 mark

Test 1 total marks ..../8

Aural Question

1

Monday

Tuesday

Saturday

Sunday

1 mark

2 Sufia has cards that are numbered 1 to 10

She turns over three of the cards.

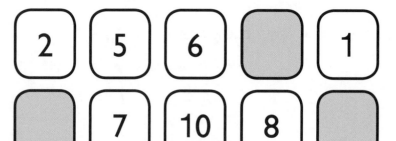

| 2 | 5 | 6 | | 1 |

| | 7 | 10 | 8 | |

Which three cards has Sufia turned over?

Write the numbers on the cards below.

1 mark

3 Write the missing numbers in the sequence.

| 40 | 35 | 30 | | | |

1 mark

4 Each pair of counters has a **total of 50**

Write numbers to complete the pairs.

One is done for you.

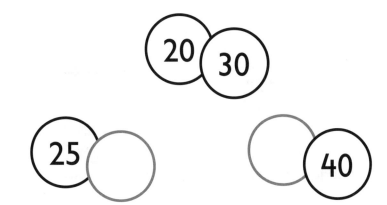

1 mark

5 Grace is pointing at the tree.

She turns a **full turn**.

Tick the shape Grace is pointing at after the full turn.

1 mark

6 Jack has **ten** toy cars.

Sufia has **six times** that number.

How many toy cars does Sufia have?

toy cars

7 There are **100g** of sugar in the jar.

Jack uses **45g**.

Sufia uses **15g**.

How many grams of sugar are **left** in the jar?

Show your working	
	g

2 marks

8 Leo has **85** crayons.

He gives away **48** crayons.

How many crayons does Leo have **left**?

crayons

1 mark

Aural Question

1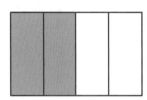

○ 1 mark

2 Write the missing numbers in the sequence.

| 24 | 22 | 20 | | | |

○ 1 mark

3 Match each clock to the time it shows.

half past three

quarter to ten

quarter past two

○ 1 mark

4 Write the next number sentence in the pattern.

$$1 + 2 + 3 = 6$$

$$1 + 2 + 4 = 7$$

$$1 + 2 + 5 = 8$$

$$1 + 2 + 6 = 9$$

☐ + ☐ + ☐ = ☐

1 mark

5 This chart shows how the children in Year 2 travelled to school today.

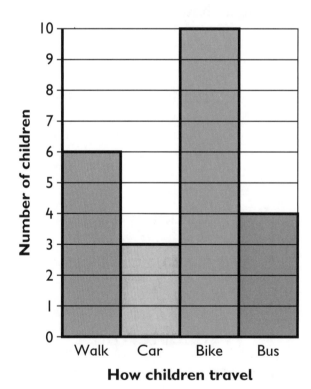

More children travelled to school on a bike than in a car.

How many more?

children

1 mark

6 A bookshelf holds 16 books.

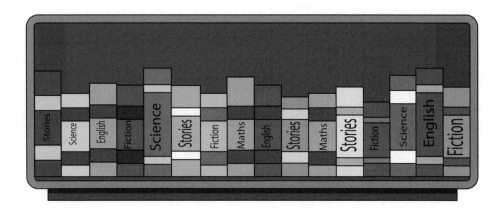

$\frac{1}{4}$ of the books are taken off the shelf to be read.

How many books are taken off the shelf?

books

1 mark

7 Sufia has **72** book tokens.

She uses **27** book tokens to buy a book.

How many book tokens does Sufia have **left**?

book tokens

1 mark

8 Jack has **70p**.

He buys **2** stickers.

Each sticker costs **15p**.

How much money does Jack have **left**?

Show your working

p

2 marks

Aural Question

1

$$14 = \boxed{} \times 7$$

○ 1 mark

---

2 Circle the **three** cards that add up to 15

○ 1 mark

3 Write the correct number in the box.

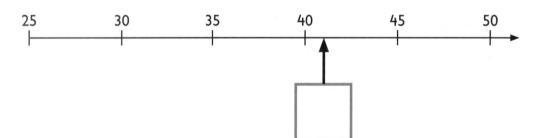

○ 1 mark

4 Meera has **£1**

She buys a pen for **45p**.

Tick the bag that shows how much Meera has **left**.

○ 1 mark

5 Here is a cuboid.

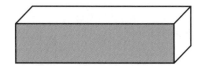

Circle **all** the shapes that are faces on this cuboid.

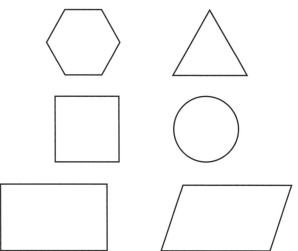

1 mark

6 Sufia has four digit cards.

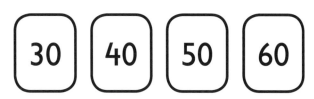

Use **three** of her cards to make these correct.

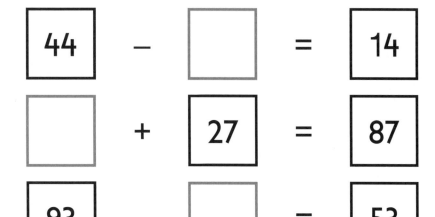

2 marks

7 Jack plays a maths game.

Each  is equal to **3** points.

 + + = **10 points**

How many points is **one** equal to?

points

1 mark

8 Write **five** coins that have a total of **42p**

P	P	P	P	P

1 mark

Test 4 total marks ..../9

Aural Question

1

67

1 mark

---

2 Match each shape to its correct description.

One is done for you.

shape

cube

triangular prism

cylinder

sphere

description

has six square faces

has two circular faces

has one face

has two triangular faces and three rectangular faces

1 mark

3 Match each box of chocolates to the correct multiplication.

One is done for you.

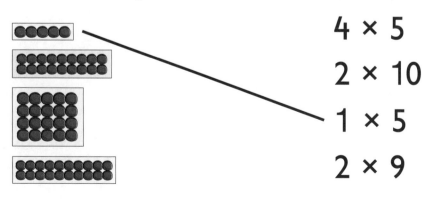

4 × 5

2 × 10

1 × 5

2 × 9

1 mark

4 Jack has cards that are numbered between 50 and 100

He turns over five of the cards.

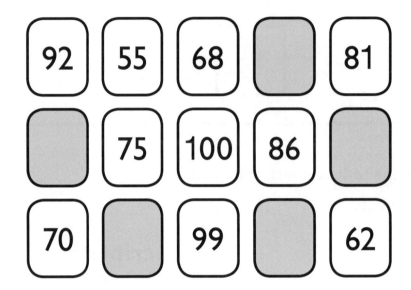

Which five cards **could** Jack have turned over?

Write the numbers on the cards below.

5 Complete the number sentences.

One is done for you.

$$\frac{1}{4} \text{ of } \boxed{16} = 4$$

$$\frac{1}{4} \text{ of } \boxed{} = 5$$

6 Write six coins that have a total of 59p.

p	p	p	p	p	p

1 mark

7 There are **100g** of butter in a dish.

Sufia uses **44g**.

Jack uses **26g**.

How many grams of butter are **left** in the dish?

Show your working

g

2 marks

8 Sufia has **94** stickers.

She gives **39** stickers away.

How many stickers does Sufia have **left**?

stickers

1 mark

Test 5 total marks ..../9

Aural Question

1

90 ☐ 100

1 mark

---

2 Circle the **three** jigsaw pieces that add up to 19

1 mark

3 Complete the number sentences.

One is done for you.

$$\frac{2}{4} \text{ of } \boxed{12} = 6$$

$$\frac{2}{4} \text{ of } \boxed{} = 8$$

1 mark

4 Tick the shape that has a line of symmetry.

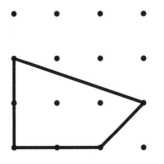 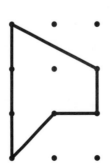 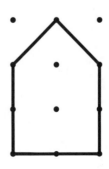 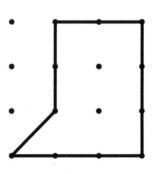

1 mark

5 Jack has **10** building blocks.

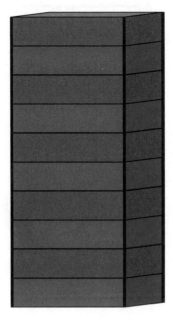

Sufia has **five times** that number.

How many building blocks does Sufia have?

building blocks

1 mark

6 Mo has **50** strawberries.

He shares them equally between **5** friends.

Jack   Sufia   Grace   Leo   Meera

Complete the number sentence to show how Mo shares the strawberries.

1 mark

7 Put a **digit** into each empty box to make the calculation correct.

$$\boxed{}\,\boxed{5} \;+\; \boxed{2}\,\boxed{} \;=\; \boxed{38}$$

1 mark

8 Sufia has **80p**.

She buys **2** pencils.

Each pencil costs **35p**.

How much money does Sufia have **left**?

Show your working

P

2 marks

Test 6 total marks ..../9

Aural Question

1

January

March

June

December

1 mark

---

2 Here are two counters.

Choose a counter to make each calculation correct.

One is done for you.

8 (+) 1 = 9   24 ( ) 1 = 25

30 ( ) 1 = 29   49 ( ) 1 = 50

1 mark

3 Each pair of cards has a **total of 90**

Write numbers to complete the pairs.

One is done for you.

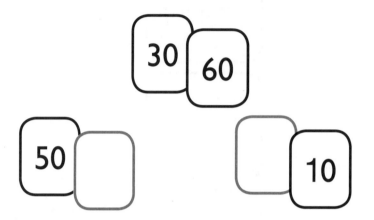

4 Write the correct number in the box.

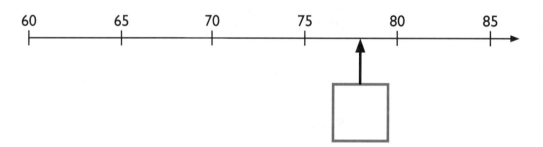

5 Sufia has £1

She buys a ruler for **65p**.

Tick the bag that shows how much Sufia has **left**.

6 Some children made a chart of how many times they ran around a track in ten minutes.

Key: stands for **1** lap

Jack	🏃 🏃
Sufia	🏃 🏃 🏃 🏃
Leo	🏃 🏃 🏃 🏃 🏃
Meera	🏃 🏃

Which children ran more than 3 laps?

Circle them.

Jack   Sufia   Leo   Meera

○ 1 mark

7 Jack has **£1**

He buys **2** bouncy balls.

Each bouncy ball costs **45p**.

How much money does Jack have **left**?

Show your working

P

○ 2 marks

41

8 A shop has 20 plants.

$\frac{3}{4}$ of the plants are sold by the shop.

How many plants were sold by the shop?

plants

1 mark

Aural Question

1

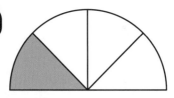 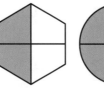 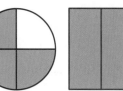

1 mark

2 Match each tray of plants to the correct multiplication.

One is done for you.

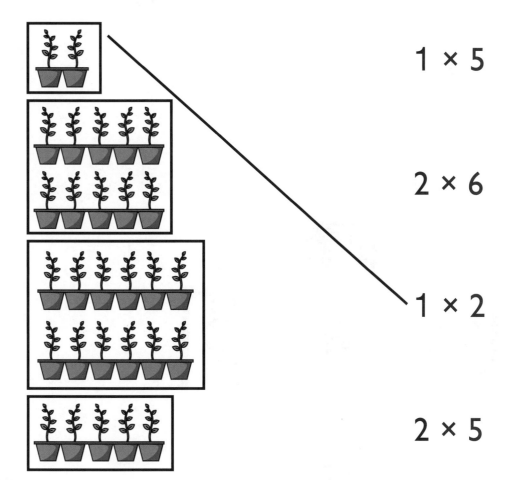

1×5

2×6

1×2

2×5

1 mark

3 Match each clock to the time it shows.

five to eleven

twenty to five

ten past two

1 mark

4 Write the next number sentence in the pattern.

$$1 + 2 + 3 = 6$$
$$1 + 3 + 4 = 8$$
$$1 + 4 + 5 = 10$$
$$1 + 5 + 6 = 12$$

☐ + ☐ + ☐ = ☐

1 mark

5 Jess is pointing at the window.

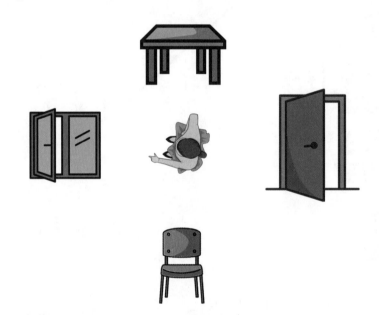

She turns **three quarters of a turn clockwise**.

Tick the object Jess is pointing at after three quarters of a turn clockwise.

1 mark

6 Sufia plays a maths game.

Each  is equal to **4** points.

 = **16 points**

How many points is **one** equal to?

| points |

○ 1 mark

7 Put a **digit** into each empty digit card to make the calculation correct.

| 2 | | **+** | | 1 | **=** | 40 |

○ 1 mark

8 There are **100g** of flour in the bag.

Jack uses **52g**.

Sufia uses **38g**.

How many grams of flour are **left** in the bag?

Flour
100g

Show your working

| g |

○ 2 marks

10 min

Sun, sea and sand

Lena sat on the beach with a frown on her face.

"You must put sun cream on, Lena," said her mum.

Lena didn't like sun cream. It felt horrible and sticky. But she knew that she had to wear it.

---

1 What is the girl's name?

_____

1 mark

2 Why was she frowning?

_____

_____

1 mark

Reading Test 1

t was very hot at the beach. The sun was beating down from a blue sky. Lena's mum did not want Lena to get burned.

Eventually, Lena agreed to put sun cream on and was soon playing in the sand and the sea. t was a glorious day.

3 Where were Lena and her mum?

Tick **one**.

on holiday ☐   on the beach ☐

in the sea ☐   at home ☐

◯ 1 mark

4 Why did Lena's mum want Lena to wear sun cream?

_____

_____

◯ 1 mark

5 **Find** and **copy one** word used to describe the day.

_____

◯ 1 mark

Test 1 total marks ..../5

Getting a pet dog

Dogs make great pets. They are quite easy to train and quickly become a well-loved member of the family.

If you would like a pet dog, there are lots of things to consider because all breeds (types) of dog are different. Some breeds need lots of exercise and space to run around. Others are fine in smaller homes. Most dogs like to be around children.

---

1 Which **two** things make dogs great pets?

Tick **two**.

They are quite easy to train. ☐   They eat a lot. ☐

They are all different. ☐   Most like to be around children. ☐

1 mark

2 Give **one** possible difference between different breeds of dog.

_____

_____

1 mark

Reading Test 2

Before getting a pet dog, ask yourself these questions:

- Is your house big enough?
- Do you have time for a dog?
- Where will you walk your dog?
- Can you afford to keep a dog?

Remember, your dog will need feeding. It will want to play too. Most dogs need exercise – at least one good walk each day. Will you want to do this when it is raining or cold?

You must also remember that a cute puppy will grow into an adult. It will still be a lovely dog but not quite as small and cute as it once was!

---

3   Draw **three** lines to match each piece of text to the main idea.

Text

Is your house big enough?

Your dog will need feeding.

It will want to play.

Idea

cost of keeping a dog

time to look after a dog

size of the dog

1 mark

4   Why does a dog need at least one good walk each day?

_____

1 mark

5   Why does the text ask, *Will you want to do this when it is raining or cold?*

_____

_____

1 mark

Test 2 total marks ..../5

The dark lake

White mist floated over the black water. It was the first time Zed had been here for two years. Ever since he heard about a horrible creature living here, he had been too afraid. He knew those dark waters hid a secret. A secret he now wanted to find out.

---

1 Which words explain why Zed had not been to the lake for two years?

_____   1 mark

2 Why was Zed at the lake now?

_____   1 mark

It was the strange man who had told Zed about the creature: a giant, winged toad. A toad that scared anybody who came too close. The man had told Zed that the toad would vanish if anybody was to stare into its eyes. Zed wanted to know if the story was true. And with the giant toad out of the way, maybe he would discover treasure in the muddy, shallow waters.

---

3 What does the text tell us about the lake?

Tick **two**.

It was shallow. ☐   A strange man lived there. ☐

It was full of treasure. ☐   It was muddy. ☐

1 mark

Zed found a large tree trunk at the edge of the water to steady himself and to hide behind.

Taking his torch from his backpack, the boy bravely shone the bright light at the lake. He leaned back against the tree and waited.

4 Think about the **whole story**.

Put ticks in the table to show which sentences are **true** and which are **false**.

Sentence	True	False
He had heard that a giant toad lived in the lake.		
It was five years since Zed had been to the lake.		
Zed carried a backpack.		

1 mark

5 What was Zed waiting for?

_____

_____

1 mark

Test 3 total marks ....**/5**

Snowy days

During the winter, we often get some snow. It might last for a few hours or a few days. It can be lots of fun to play in. There are some great things to do outside on a snowy day.

Remember to wrap up warm so you can play out for longer. Gloves and a hat are important. It is also a good idea to wear a waterproof coat and boots.

---

1 How long does the text say snow could last for?

Tick **one**.

a few days ☐   a few months ☐

all winter ☐   a few years ☐

○ 1 mark

2 Why does the text say you should wrap up warm?

_____

○ 1 mark

Building a snowman

Start with a small snowball and roll it around until it makes a large, round snowman body. Make a smaller ball for the head. Use a carrot for a nose and stones for eyes. You could use sticks for arms.

---

3 Which of these items are **not** suggested in the text for building a snowman?

Tick **one**.

sticks ☐   hat ☐

stones ☐   carrot ☐

○ 1 mark

Reading Test 4

Sledging and snowballs

You will need a sledge and a hill to slide down. Make sure there is nothing to crash into! Start on a gentle slope to practise turning and stopping. When you are ready, try a steeper hill.

Snowballs are fun to make and fun to throw. Make a small pile of snowballs and aim at a target. This could be something in your garden or in the park. Snowball fights with friends can be exciting too, but you must never aim for the head.

4   Give **two** pieces of safety advice from the text for sledging and snowballing.

1. _____

2. _____   ◯ 1 mark

Snow can be fun, but it can also cause problems.

You might like to help people by clearing snow from their path. Or you could check on elderly neighbours to make sure they have enough food in the house.

5   Why might you check on an elderly person to make sure they have enough food?

     Tick **one**.

They might need a cup of tea. ☐   Their car could be stuck. ☐

The snow might stop them from going shopping. ☐   They might be cold. ☐   ◯ 1 mark

Test 4 total marks ..../5

Blue goes missing

Jasmin loved her teddy. She called it Blue. It was given to her by her grandad for her second birthday.

One day, Jasmin and her big brother went to a museum. Of course, Blue went along too, peeping out of Jasmin's brother's bag. They looked at famous paintings, old pots, and model dinosaurs. It was a fantastic place.

At lunchtime, Jasmin's brother took a picnic from his bag. Of course, Blue also came out of the bag. They sat on the grass under a sky that was as blue as the teddy's eyes and the ribbon round its neck.

When they had finished eating, Jasmin put their litter in the bin. Her brother picked up his bag. But Blue was left sitting on the grass. Nobody noticed except an old lady, who picked up the teddy and tried to catch up with the children.

In the afternoon, Jasmin and her brother looked at old bikes and cars in the museum. The old lady tried to follow but could not quite keep up.

At the end of the day they caught the bus home. The old lady missed the bus. Jasmin reached inside the bag for Blue. Her heart sank and tears rolled down her cheeks. She could not stop crying. Her brother did not know what to do.

As the bus stopped near their house, Jasmin slowly stepped off. Behind the bus, an old lady climbed out of a taxi.

Reading Test 5

1 **Find** and **copy one** word which tells you that the museum was good.

_____ ◯ 1 mark

2 Put ticks in the table to show which sentences are **true** and which are **false**.

Sentence	True	False
Jasmin and her big brother went to a museum.		
They looked at old bikes and cars.		
The old lady got on the bus.		
Jasmin's brother bought lunch from the shop.		

◯ 2 marks

3 Number the following events from 1 to 4 to show the order that things happened in the story.

The first one has been done for you.

Jasmin slowly got off the bus. ☐

Jasmin called her teddy Blue. ⊡ 1

An old lady picked up Blue. ☐

They looked at model dinosaurs. ☐

◯ 1 mark

4 Which words tell you Jasmin was sad?

Tick **one**.

Jasmin was scared. ☐   She missed Blue. ☐

Her heart sank. ☐   How would she sleep? ☐

◯ 1 mark

5 What do you think will happen next in the story?

_____ ◯ 1 mark

Test 5 total marks ..../6

Water fun

Most people have water close to where they live. The sea, a lake, a river or even your local swimming pool are great places for fun and exercise.

There are lots of different activities to try in, on or next to the water.

In the water: swimming

The local pool is a great place to start. Swimming is an easy way to enjoy water and a fantastic way to keep fit. It is a good idea to learn to swim and to be confident in and around water. This will help you to stay safe when doing other watersports. Once you improve enough, you could try swimming in the sea or a lake.

On the water: sailing, surfing, rowing and paddle sports

Is there a sailing club near where you live? Most clubs will give you the chance to try sailing. You do not need your own boat.

There are lots of places to paddle a canoe or row a rowing boat. There are clubs that take their sport very seriously, but there are also places to paddle and row for pleasure. Give it a go and see if you enjoy it!

You need waves for surfing, so the sea is the ideal place. You will need a surfboard; you can hire a surfboard (and a wetsuit if you like) at many surfing beaches. Lessons are often available. You will need great balance. Be prepared to get very wet!

Next to the water: fishing

You can try fishing in lots of places (except your local swimming pool!). Try finding a club to help you at first. They can tell you where to go fishing and lend you the equipment.

Big Tips

- Make sure you are with an adult.
- Wear a life jacket when needed.
- Do not go out of your depth.
- Check for dangers.

Learning to swim in an indoor pool

Sailing on the sea

Surfing: be prepared to get very wet!

Fishing in a river

Reading Test 6

1 Look at the section with the title, *In the water: swimming.*

Find and **copy one** word from this section used to indicate getting better at swimming.

_____

1 mark

2 Which of these do you **not** need for surfing?

Tick **one**.

balance ☐   a surfboard ☐

waves ☐   a wetsuit ☐

1 mark

3 Name **two** different places mentioned in the text to try water activities.

1. _____

2. _____

1 mark

4 What is the purpose of the information in the *Big Tips* box?

_____

1 mark

5 Give **two** reasons why you think swimming is the first activity mentioned.

1. _____

2. _____

2 marks

Test 6 total marks ..../6

Paint a picture

Sad or happy, give your brain a stretch,

Your mood can be your starting sketch.

Then paint a picture in your mind,

And leave the real world behind.

Think of a strange or exciting scene,

Eating blue chocolate, or meeting the queen.

Add more detail, do not rush,

Your imagination is your brush.

Travel near, travel far,

The local park or a distant star.

Be who or what, you decide,

Allow your thoughts to be your guide.

So when you think you need a break,

Think rainbow ice-creams, or a spotty snake.

Disappear without a trace,

Into your picture, your special place.

Reading Test 7

1   **Find** and **copy two** words that show what mood you could be in.

1. _____

2. _____

○ 1 mark

2   Where does the poem suggest you paint your picture?

         Tick **one**.

in the park ☐   in your mind ☐

on a star ☐   at home ☐

○ 1 mark

3   Draw **three lines** to show what the poem links with different parts of painting a picture.

starting sketch		your imagination
guide		your mood
paintbrush		your thoughts

○ 1 mark

4   **Find** and **copy** the words in the last verse which tell you that the picture is just for you.

_____

○ 1 mark

5   Why does the text make suggestions about strange ideas such as *blue chocolate, rainbow ice-creams* or a *spotty snake*?

_____

_____

○ 2 marks

Test 7 total marks ..../6

59

Cheese roll anyone?

Every spring, near the city of Gloucester, a very strange competition takes place. On Cooper's Hill, locals are joined by people from all over the world. They come to take part in an event that first took place hundreds of years ago. It is now a famous tradition.

Gloucester is well-known for its cheese and also for cheese rolling! At the end of May each year, cheese rollers gather at the top of Cooper's Hill. Each competitor then chases a huge, round Double Gloucester cheese from the top of the hill to the bottom. The winner is the first person to cross the line behind the cheese.

Cheese rolling on Cooper's Hill, Gloucester

The slope is steep and the race is fast. Many people end up tumbling down the hillside and, unfortunately, some get injured.

Imagine the sight of lots of people chasing a cheese down a hillside! It must be great fun to watch!

A race winner with the cheese

Reading Test 8

1 This text is about:

Tick **one**.

making cheese ☐   a running race ☐

hills ☐   cheese rolling ☐

◯ 1 mark

2 When did this event first take place?

_____

◯ 1 mark

3 What type of cheese is used?

_____

◯ 1 mark

4 Why do you think it is important that the cheese is round?

_____

◯ 1 mark

5 What makes cheese rolling dangerous? Explain your answer.

_____

_____

◯ 2 marks

Test 8 total marks ..../6

61

10 min

1 Tick the correct word to complete the sentence below.

Samia was hungry _____ she had not eaten any breakfast.

Tick **one**.

so ☐

and ☐

because ☐

or ☐

1 mark

2 Circle the **noun** in the sentence below.

There was a huge elephant eating.

1 mark

3 Add a **full stop** or a **question mark** to complete each sentence below.

When will the show start ☐

Make sure you eat your lunch ☐

Was it a long journey ☐

1 mark

4 What type of word is <u>buzzing</u> in the sentence below?

A small fly was <u>buzzing</u> around Ava's head.

Tick **one**.

an adjective

a noun

a verb

an adverb

○ 1 mark

5 Circle the **adjective** in the sentence below.

Jack   looked   up   as   the   amazing   balloon   drifted   past.

○ 1 mark

6 Which sentence is written in the **present tense**?

Tick **one**.

The dogs played in the garden.

The dogs went for a walk.

The dogs are making a loud noise.

The dogs ran after the ball.

○ 1 mark

Grammar and Punctuation Test 1

7 Add a **comma** in the correct place in the sentence below.

We need to buy bread cheese and cake.

1 mark

8 Write one word to complete the sentence below.

You can eat your lunch outside _____ it is not raining.

1 mark

9 Write **one** sentence to describe something you see in the picture.

Remember to use the correct punctuation.

_____

_____

2 marks

Test 1 total marks ..../10

1 What type of word is <u>motorbike</u> in the sentence below?

A very fast <u>motorbike</u> zoomed past.

Tick **one**.

a verb ☐

an adverb ☐

an adjective ☐

a noun ☐

◯
1 mark

2 Circle the **verb** in the sentence below.

All   the   children   danced   at   the   school   disco.

◯
1 mark

3 Which sentence is punctuated correctly?

Tick **one**.

Jade walks home every Friday. ☐

Jade walks home every Friday ☐

jade walks Home every Friday. ☐

Jade walks home. Every Friday. ☐

◯
1 mark

4 Tick the name of the punctuation mark that should complete each sentence.

Sentence	Full stop	Question mark
Where is the train station		
The train will be here soon		
When I get on the train, I will read		

1 mark

5 What type of sentence is below? The end punctuation is covered.

What an incredible sunset we saw

Tick **one**.

a command ☐

a question ☐

an exclamation ☐

a statement ☐

1 mark

6 Add two letters to the word <u>welcome</u> to make a word that means <u>not welcome</u>.

The teacher said they should not be in the room.
They felt they were ___welcome.

1 mark

7 Circle the word that shows the sentence below is in the **past tense**.

Amy   had   a   very   good   day   at   school.

1 mark

8 Write **one** verb to complete the sentence about what each person is doing.

Last week, Ethan _____ football.

Today, Katie is _____ football.

2 marks

9 Write a **command** a parent could say to their child who has a messy bedroom.

Remember to use correct punctuation.

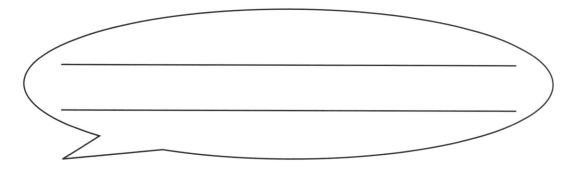

2 marks

1 What type of word is <u>slowly</u> in the sentence below?

The boat chugged <u>slowly</u> along the river.

Tick **one**.

a verb ☐

an adverb ☐

an adjective ☐

a noun ☐

 1 mark

2 Circle **one** word in the sentence below that can be replaced by the word <u>when</u>.

We are always excited if Uncle Jack is visiting.

 1 mark

3 Tick to show whether each word is an **adjective** or an **adverb**.

Word	Adjective	Adverb
slow		
quickly		
carefully		

 1 mark

4 Tick the **noun phrase** below.

Tick **one**.

running fast ☐

a small sandwich ☐

eaten lunch ☐

tired out ☐

1 mark

5 Add **two full stops** in the correct places below.

Anna had lots of sweets Seb asked her to share them

1 mark

6 Which sentence is written in the **past tense**?

Tick **one**.

Leah is running home. ☐

Leah is running fast. ☐

Leah had lunch at school. ☐

Leah is at school. ☐

1 mark

7 Tick the **two nouns** in the sentence below.

They painted a wonderful picture on the wall.

☐   ☐   ☐   ☐

1 mark

8 Which sentence uses an **exclamation mark** correctly?

Tick **one**.

What do you want to draw! ☐

What a brilliant picture you have painted! ☐

How did you do that! ☐

Did you work hard! ☐

1 mark

9 Write **one** sentence to describe this house.

Remember to use the correct punctuation.

_____

_____

2 marks

Test 3 total marks ..../10

10 min

1 Tick **one** word to complete the sentence below.

Playing in the sea can be great fun, _____ you must make sure it is safe.

Tick **one**.

when ☐

or ☐

but ☐

that ☐

1 mark

2 Add a suffix to the word <u>quick</u> in the sentence below to make an **adverb**.

The cat was running quick____ to escape the rain.

1 mark

3 Tick the sentence which shows what the children are doing <u>now</u>.

Tick **one**.

The children did their work. ☐

The children are doing some maths. ☐

The children played in the sand. ☐

The children jumped up and down. ☐

1 mark

4 The sentences below have their punctuation covered.

Which sentence is a **question**?

Tick **one**.

What an amazing story this is ▮ ☐

How colourful that bird is ▮ ☐

How I would love a holiday ▮ ☐

What kind of books do you read ▮ ☐

1 mark

5 Circle **one** word in the sentence below that can be replaced by the word <u>but</u>.

Dav had ice-cream at the theatre and Jen had popcorn.

1 mark

6 Which punctuation is needed in the sentence below?

Tommy likes music running and rugby.

Tick **one**.

a question mark ☐

an exclamation mark ☐

an apostrophe ☐

a comma ☐

1 mark

7 Add an **apostrophe** in the correct place in the sentence below.

Here is Mums new car.

1 mark

8 Complete the sentence below by adding two letters to the word *healthy* to show that eating sweets is not healthy.

Sweets are full of sugar and eating them is _____.

1 mark

9 Write **one** sentence about the girl in the picture that includes a verb.

Remember to use the correct punctuation.

_____

_____

2 marks

1 What type of word is <u>bright</u> in the sentence below?

As they looked up at the sky, they saw a <u>bright</u> star.

Tick **one**.

an adverb ☐

a noun ☐

an adjective ☐

a verb ☐

1 mark

2 Circle all the **verbs** in the sentence below.

Sam   cleaned   the   car   while   Jess   checked   the   engine.

1 mark

3 Which sentence below uses a **comma** correctly?

Tick **one**.

The river, was long and wide. ☐

Red and green fireworks, lit the sky. ☐

My favourite fruits are, apples and pears. ☐

We run, jump and skip as fast as we can. ☐

1 mark

4 Tick to show whether each sentence is in the **past tense** or the **present tense**.

Sentence	Past tense	Present tense
I went on holiday to Spain.		
Pavel is hiding under the stairs.		
Erin drew a picture of a rocket.		

1 mark

5 Circle **one** noun in the sentence below that is **plural**.

They had a dog, a cat, rabbits and a large house.

1 mark

6 Look at where the arrow is pointing. Which punctuation mark is needed?

Sami looked everywhere for the cat but could not find it

Tick **one**.

a question mark ☐

a comma ☐

a full stop ☐

an apostrophe ☐

1 mark

Grammar and Punctuation Test 5

7 Which sentence needs more than one **capital letter**?

Tick **one**.

their new house was large. ☐

luca's cousin is from italy. ☐

i go swimming every week. ☐

javed has a large, red bike. ☐

1 mark

8 Use only the words in the box below to write a **statement**.

| big | is | garden | the |

Remember to use the correct punctuation.

_____

2 marks

9 Write a question you could ask if you wanted to know the time.

Remember to use the correct punctuation.

_____

2 marks

Test 5 total marks ..../11

1 What is the sentence below? The end punctuation is covered.

Move that bike out of the way

Tick **one**.

an exclamation ☐

a question ☐

a command ☐

a statement ☐

○
1 mark

2 Circle **one** word in the sentence below that can be replaced with the word <u>or</u>.

She could not decide whether to have salad and chips with her meal.

○
1 mark

3 Tick the **two adverbs** in the sentence below.

Carefully, they jumped onto the rock as the water quietly flowed by.

☐   ☐   ☐   ☐

○
1 mark

4 Which punctuation mark is needed in the sentence below?

When where and how they would travel was a mystery.

Tick **one**.

a comma ☐

an exclamation mark ☐

an apostrophe ☐

a question mark ☐

1 mark

5 Circle all the **verbs** in the sentence below.

Harry picked many apples and carefully placed them in large boxes.

1 mark

6 Circle **one** word in the sentence below that can be replaced with the word <u>but</u>.

We enjoy going on bike rides although we only cycle in the summer.

1 mark

7 Write the words <u>would not</u> as one word, using an **apostrophe**.

The cat <u>would not</u> come down from the tree.

8 Rewrite the verb in the box to complete the sentence in the correct **tense**.

The children _____ their lunch and went outside to play.

| eat |

9 Write **one** verb to complete what each child is saying.

Yesterday, I _____ a cake.

Today, I am _____ a cake.

Test 6 total marks ..../10

1 What type of word is <u>lovely</u> in the sentence below?

It was a <u>lovely</u> day to go to the beach.

Tick **one**.

a noun ☐

an adjective ☐

an adverb ☐

a verb ☐

1 mark

2 Circle **one** word in the sentence below that can be replaced with the word <u>but</u>.

Ava was watching the television and Stefan was sleeping.

1 mark

3 Draw a line to match each word to the **suffix** that turns it into a noun.

Word

sad

entertain

kind

Suffix

ness

ment

ness

ment

ness

ment

1 mark

4 Tick the sentence that shows what Dan will do <u>later</u>.

Tick **one**.

Dan is doing the ironing. ☐

Dan went to the shops. ☐

Dan will make dinner. ☐

Dan made lunch. ☐

1 mark

5 Circle the **two** words that need a **capital letter** in the sentence below.

yesterday, emma went to the river with her dog.

1 mark

6 Tick the correct option to complete the sentence below.

_____ invite everyone to the party.

Tick **one**.

Theyll' ☐

The'yll ☐

They'll ☐

Theyl'l ☐

1 mark

Grammar and Punctuation Test 7

7 Tick to show whether each noun is **singular** or **plural**.

Noun	Singular	Plural
mice		
animals		
person		

1 mark

8 Why does the word <u>Spain</u> start with a capital letter in the sentence below?

Tommy and Lena flew to <u>Spain</u> for their holiday.

_____

1 mark

9 Write one sentence to describe something you see in the picture.

Remember to use the correct punctuation.

_____

_____

2 marks

Test 7 total marks ..../10

10 min

1 Look at the word below.

helpful

Which word below changes the meaning to **not helpful**?

Tick **one**.

helpless ☐

helping ☐

unhelpful ☐

helper ☐

1 mark

2 The sentence below should all be in the **past tense**.

Circle **one** word that needs to be changed.

When she finished her homework she practises her drumming.

1 mark

3 What type of word is <u>delicious</u> in the sentence below?

Ryley likes to eat <u>delicious</u> bread from the bakery.

Tick **one**.

a verb ☐

a noun ☐

an adjective ☐

an adverb ☐

1 mark

4 Tick to show whether each sentence is in the **past tense** or the **present tense**.

Sentence	Past tense	Present tense
They are eating their favourite food.		
Annie is playing the piano.		
We have made a wooden doll.		

1 mark

5 Add a **question mark** in the correct place below.

When would they get home Ali was feeling tired.

1 mark

6 What is needed in the sentence below?

when it was over, Jack jumped for joy.

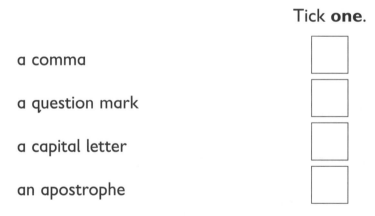

Tick **one**.

a comma ☐

a question mark ☐

a capital letter ☐

an apostrophe ☐

1 mark

7 Circle **one** word in the sentence below that can be replaced by the word <u>then</u>.

Eat your vegetables so you can have some cake.

1 mark

8 Tick **two** words that can have the letters <u>ful</u> at the end to make another word.

Tick **two**.

sad ☐

some ☐

help ☐

use ☐

1 mark

9 Write an **exclamation** you could say if you saw an amazing picture.

Remember to use correct punctuation.

_____

_____

2 marks

Test 8 total marks ..../10

Spelling Test 1

1 The rabbit lives in a _____ .

1 mark

2 We _____ into the swimming pool.

1 mark

3 I changed into my PE _____ .

1 mark

4 The house was _____ the shops.

1 mark

5 There are _____ cakes at Gran's house.

1 mark

6 Her new watch has a _____ strap.

1 mark

7 He was not hurt _____ when he fell.

1 mark

8 We watched a _____ show at the circus.

1 mark

9 Olivia will soon have a new _____ .

1 mark

10 The _____ smashed on the floor.

1 mark

Test 1 total marks ..../10

1 Turn _____ at the next junction.

○ 1 mark

2 London is a large _____ .

○ 1 mark

3 Sara _____ she could not play today.

○ 1 mark

4 The train went through a long _____ .

○ 1 mark

5 It was the _____ dance they had ever seen.

○ 1 mark

6 The children had to _____ the car.

○ 1 mark

7 My friend was on the _____ side of the road.

○ 1 mark

8 Freya took her _____ to throw the ball.

○ 1 mark

9 Mum hurt her _____ playing netball.

○ 1 mark

10 They used a towel to _____ themselves.

○ 1 mark

Test 2 total marks ..../10

10 min

1. The class had to _____ a story.

1 mark

2. Kenji's favourite _____ is the giraffe.

1 mark

3. Somebody left the tap running in the _____ .

1 mark

4. Jess had a very strange _____ .
1 mark

5. We _____ we will visit the museum tomorrow.
1 mark

6. Each week, they _____ to charity.

1 mark

7. For his birthday, Owen got a _____ .

1 mark

8. The train was late leaving the _____ .

1 mark

9. Amy waited for her _____ .
1 mark

10. Liam had a new _____ .
1 mark

Test 3 total marks ..../10

10 min

1 Dad wiped the dirt _____ his shoes.

1 mark

2 The children played in the _____ .

1 mark

3 Mum has to _____ far to work.

1 mark

4 Smoke was coming from the _____ .

1 mark

5 A _____ of the roof was leaking.

1 mark

6 He could hear the _____ of his own breathing.

1 mark

7 They went to their _____ holiday destination.

1 mark

8 Mum decided that we _____ leave soon.

1 mark

9 I _____ brush my teeth at bedtime.

1 mark

10 It was amazing to see a _____ in the harbour.

1 mark

Test 4 total marks ..../10

1 The children were _____ in the library.

1 mark

2 All of the players walked onto the _____ .

1 mark

3 The benches were all made of _____ .

1 mark

4 The rescued tiger was put in a _____ .

1 mark

5 We went to see the film _____ .

1 mark

6 Everybody _____ at the school disco.

1 mark

7 Stevie put the bread in his _____ .

1 mark

8 The children had a drink of orange _____ .

1 mark

9 There was great _____ when the teacher retired.

1 mark

10 Mo heard the _____ at the door.

1 mark

Test 5 total marks ..../10

Spelling Test 6

1 The geese all flew _____ home.

1 mark

2 It was _____ in the cinema.

1 mark

3 The _____ was very fast.

1 mark

4 _____ the bed is a box of secrets.

1 mark

5 It took ages to _____ the journey.

1 mark

6 Mrs Smith _____ a meal.

1 mark

7 The _____ was on all day.

1 mark

8 _____ insects covered the plants.

1 mark

9 Jane helped me tie my _____ .

1 mark

10 He knew it was _____ so he said sorry.

1 mark

Test 6 total marks ..../10

10 min

1 The class assembly made everyone _____ .

1 mark

2 The go-kart lost a _____ on the hill.

1 mark

3 We all did _____ in the tests.

1 mark

4 The paintings were found in a hidden _____ .

1 mark

5 I could not find my _____ at the football match.

1 mark

6 Harry found the _____ way to the lake.

1 mark

7 I only got one _____ wrong in my spellings.

1 mark

8 It is believed that the _____ was hidden nearby.

1 mark

9 They only went shopping in _____ shops.

1 mark

10 It is _____ to walk to school sometimes.

1 mark

Test 7 total marks ..../10

10 min

1 Her best photograph was of a _____ .

1 mark

2 Millie had a rash on her _____ .

1 mark

3 I did not know _____ the car was parked.

1 mark

4 There were many hiding places in the _____ .

1 mark

5 They went to the _____ to get some money.

1 mark

6 The ugly duckling turned into a beautiful _____ .

1 mark

7 There was _____ they could do to help.

1 mark

8 Lou was the fastest _____ in the school.

1 mark

9 The whole team _____ really hard.

1 mark

10 We found a _____ in the duck pond.

1 mark

Test 8 total marks ..../10

Answers

Arithmetic

Question	Requirement	Mark
Test 1		
1	5	1
2	19	1
3	12	1
4	66	1
5	40	1
6	9	1
7	57	1
8	62	1
9	23	1
10	2	1
11	35	1
12	67	1
Test 2		
1	19	1
2	13	1
3	30	1
4	120	1
5	104	1
6	25	1
7	5	1
8	85	1
9	3	1
10	27	1
11	22	1
12	36	1
Test 3		
1	4	1
2	18	1
3	88	1
4	30	1
5	90	1
6	13	1
7	18	1
8	4	1
9	41	1

Question	Requirement	Mark
10	14	1
11	62	1
12	85	1
Test 4		
1	20	1
2	10	1
3	12	1
4	45	1
5	27	1
6	8	1
7	29	1
8	23	1
9	67	1
10	5	1
11	90	1
12	25	1
Test 5		
1	12	1
2	102	1
3	13	1
4	30	1
5	88	1
6	24	1
7	11	1
8	80	1
9	40	1
10	6	1
11	10	1
12	57	1
Test 6		
1	20	1
2	30	1
3	47	1
4	107	1
5	80	1
6	7	1

Answers

Question	Requirement	Mark
7	97	1
8	58	1
9	2	1
10	12	1
11	90	1
12	52	1
Test 7		
1	2	1
2	20	1
3	50	1
4	102	1
5	55	1
6	11	1
7	70	1
8	7	1
9	50	1

Question	Requirement	Mark
10	58	1
11	18	1
12	7	1
Test 8		
1	57	1
2	13	1
3	38	1
4	80	1
5	86	1
6	58	1
7	9	1
8	15	1
9	62	1
10	35	1
11	14	1
12	33	1

Reasoning

The Reasoning paper of the KS1 test begins with aural questions, which are read out loud to the children (rather than the children reading the questions on the page). To provide practice for these aural questions, each of the eight Reasoning tests in this book begins with one aural question.

For each test, read the relevant question (below) out loud, allowing time for your child to write their answer. Once they have written their answer, say: *For the rest of the test, you will need to read the questions in the booklet yourself.*

Test 1
Question 1: *Write down an odd number that comes between sixty and seventy. Write the number in the box.*

Test 2
Question 1: *Look at the cards. I will read them for you: Monday, Tuesday, Saturday, Sunday. Tick the card that shows the name of the day after Friday.*

Test 3
Question 1: *Look at the five shapes. Tick all the shapes that have a quarter shaded.*

Test 4
Question 1: *Look at the calculation. Write a number in the box to make the calculation correct.*

Test 5
Question 1: *What is sixty-seven minus ten? Write your answer in the box.*

Test 6
Question 1: *Write down an even number that comes between ninety and one hundred. Write the number in the box.*

Test 7
Question 1: *Look at the cards. I will read them for you: January, March, June, December. Tick the card that shows the name of the month after November.*

Test 8
Question 1: *Look at the five shapes. Tick all the shapes that have three quarters shaded.*

Answers

Question	Requirement	Mark	Additional Guidance
Test 1			
1	61 **OR** 63 **OR** 65 **OR** 67 **OR** 69	1	
2	rectangle — has three vertices triangle — has five equal sides hexagon — has four right angles pentagon — has six vertices	1	All three must be correctly matched. **Do not** award the mark if a shape is matched to more than one description. Ignore any extra lines drawn from 'rectangle'.
3	25 **+** 1 = 26 50 **+** 1 = 51 39 **−** 1 = 38	1	All three signs must be correct. Accept slight inaccuracies in the drawing of the signs, as long as the intention is clear.
4	5 ✓ 3 ✓ 9 ✓	1	All three correct cards must be ticked. Accept any other clear way of indicating the correct cards, e.g. circling. **Do not** award the mark if more than three cards are ticked, unless it is clear that the correct three are the final answer.
5	$\frac{1}{2}$ of **12** = 6	1	
6	(sets of satsumas matched to: 3 × 2, 7 × 2, 2 × 2, 4 × 2)	1	All three sets of satsumas must be correctly matched. **Do not** award the mark if a set is matched to more than one calculation. Ignore any extra lines drawn from the first set.
7	(jar)	1	Accept any other clear way of indicating the correct jar, e.g. circling. **Do not** award the mark if more than one jar has been ticked, unless it is clear that the correct jar is the final answer.
8	40 ÷ 4 = 10	1	All three numbers must be correct. **Do not** accept 40 ÷ 10 = 4
Test 2			
1	Saturday ✓	1	Accept any other clear way of indicating the correct day, e.g. circling. **Do not** award the mark if additional days are indicated, unless it is clear that the correct day is the final answer.
2	3, 4, 9	1	All three numbers must be given. They may be in any order.
3	25, 20, 15	1	All three numbers must be correct and in the order shown.
4	(20)(30) (25)(25) (10)(40)	1	Both numbers must be correct.
5	(tree) ✓	1	Accept any other clear way of indicating the correct answer, e.g. circling. **Do not** award the mark if additional objects are ticked, unless it is clear that the correct object is the final answer.

6	60	1	**Do not** accept 6 × 10 or 10 × 6 if the answer of 60 is not given as well.
7	40g	2	Award **TWO** marks for the correct answer of 40(g). If the answer is incorrect or missing, award **ONE** mark for a complete, correct method, e.g. • 100 − 45 − 15 = (no answer) • 45 + 15 = 70 ⇨ 100 − 70 = 30 (incorrect) **OR** Any partial method carried out correctly but missing the correct answer, e.g. • 100 − 45 = 55 • 100 − 15 = 85 • 45 + 15 = 60
8	37	1	

Test 3

1		1	Both correct shapes must be ticked. Accept any other clear way of indicating the two correct shapes, e.g. circling. **Do not** award the mark if additional shapes are ticked, unless it is clear that the two correct shapes are the final answer.
2	18, 16, 14	1	All three numbers must be correct and in the order shown.
3	half past three / quarter to ten / quarter past two	1	All three clocks must be correctly matched. **Do not** award the mark if a clock face is matched to more than one time.
4	1 + 2 + 7 = 10	1	All four numbers in the number sentence must be correct and in the order shown.
5	7	1	
6	4	1	
7	45	1	
8	40p	2	Award **TWO** marks for the correct answer of 40(p). If the answer is incorrect or missing, award **ONE** mark for a complete, correct method, e.g. • 70 − 15 − 15 = (no answer) • 70 − 2 × 15 = (no answer) • 70 − 30 = (no answer) • 70 − 15 = 50 − 15 = (incorrect) • 15 × 2 = 40 ⇨ 70 − 40 (incorrect) **OR** Any partial method carried out correctly but missing the correct answer, e.g. • 15 + 15 = 30 • 15 × 2 = 30 • 70 − 15 = 55

Answers

Test 4			
1	2	1	
2	1, 8, 6	1	All three correct cards must be circled. Accept any other clear way of indicating the correct answer, e.g. ticking. **Do not** award the mark if more than three cards are circled, unless it is clear that the correct cards are the final answer.
3	41	1	Also accept 42
4	✓	1	Accept any other clear way of indicating the correct answer, e.g. circling. **Do not** award the mark if more than one bag has been ticked, unless it is clear that the correct bag is the final answer.
5		1	Both correct shapes must be circled. Accept any other clear way of indicating the correct answer, e.g. ticking. **Do not** award the mark if additional shapes are circled, unless it is clear that the correct shapes are the final answer.
6	44 − **30** = 14 **60** + 27 = 87 93 − **40** = 53	2	All three number sentences must be completed correctly for **TWO** marks. Award **ONE** mark for two number sentences completed correctly. Accept any other clear way of indicating the correct answers, e.g. matching correct cards to answer boxes.
7	4	1	
8	10p, 10p, 10p, 10p, 2p **OR** 20p, 10p, 10p, 1p, 1p **OR** 20p, 10p, 5p, 5p, 2p	1	All **five** coins must be correct. Coins may be written in any order. **Do not** award the mark if additional incorrect coins are given as part of the answer.
Test 5			
1	57	1	
2	cube ——————— has six square faces triangular prism ⟋ has two circular faces cylinder ⟋ has one face sphere ⟋ has two triangular faces and three rectangular faces	1	All three shapes must be correctly matched. **Do not** award the mark if a shape is matched to more than one description. Ignore any extra lines drawn from 'cube'.
3		1	All three boxes must be correctly matched. **Do not** award the mark if a box is matched to more than one calculation. Ignore any extra lines drawn from the first box.
4	Any five correct numbers between 50 and 100 that are not already shown on the other cards.	1	Five correct answers must be given. They may be in any order. **Do not** accept 92, 55, 68, 81, 75, 100, 86, 70, 99 or 62.

Answers

5	$\frac{1}{4}$ of **20** = 5	1	
6	20p, 20p, 10p, 5p, 2p, 2p **OR** 50p, 2p, 2p, 2p, 2p, 1p **OR** 50p, 5p, 1p, 1p, 1p, 1p	1	All **six** coins must be correct. Coins may be written in any order. **Do not** award the mark if additional incorrect coins are given as part of the answer.
7	30g	2	Award **TWO** marks for the correct answer of 30(g). If the answer is incorrect or missing, award **ONE** mark for a complete, correct method, e.g. • 100 − 44 − 26 = (no answer) • 44 + 26 = 60 ⇨ 100 − 60 = 40 (incorrect) **OR** Any partial method carried out correctly but missing the correct answer, e.g. • 100 − 44 = 56 • 100 − 26 = 74 • 44 + 26 = 70
8	55	1	

Test 6

1	92 **OR** 94 **OR** 96 **OR** 98	1	
2	9, 8, 2	1	All three correct jigsaw pieces must be circled. Accept any other clear way of indicating the correct answer, e.g. ticking. **Do not** award the mark if more than three jigsaw pieces are circled, unless it is clear that the correct jigsaw pieces are the final answer.
3	$\frac{2}{4}$ of **16** = 8	1	
4		1	Accept any other clear way of indicating the correct answer, e.g. circling. **Do not** award the mark if additional shapes are ticked, unless it is clear that the correct shape is the final answer.
5	50 (building blocks)	1	**Do not** accept 5 × 10 or 10 × 5 if the answer of 50 is not given.
6	50 ÷ 5 = 10	1	All three numbers must be correct. **Do not** accept 50 ÷ 10 = 5
7	**15** + **23** = 38	1	Both numbers in the calculation must be correct.
8	10p	2	Award **TWO** marks for the correct answer of 10(p). If the answer is incorrect or missing, award **ONE** mark for a complete, correct method, e.g. • 80 − 35 − 35 = (no answer) • 80 − 2 × 35 = (no answer) • 80 − 70 = (no answer) • 80 − 35 = 50 ⇨ 50 − 35 = 15 (incorrect) • 35 × 2 = 60 ⇨ 80 − 60 = 20 (incorrect) **OR** Any partial method carried out correctly but missing the correct answer, e.g. • 35 + 35 = 70 • 35 × 2 = 70 • 80 − 35 = 45

Answers

Test 7			
1	December ✓	1	Accept any other clear way of indicating the correct answer, e.g. circling. **Do not** award the mark if additional months are ticked, unless it is clear that the correct month is the final answer.
2	24 + 1 = 25 30 − 1 = 29 49 + 1 = 50	1	All three signs must be correct. Accept slight inaccuracies in the drawing of the signs, as long as the intention is clear.
3	30 60 50 40 80 10	1	Both numbers must be correct.
4	78	1	Also accept 77 or 79
5	✓	1	Accept any other clear way of indicating the correct answer, e.g. circling. **Do not** award the mark if more than one bag has been ticked, unless it is clear that the correct bag is the final answer.
6	Sufia, Leo	1	Accept any other clear way of indicating the two correct answers, e.g. ticking. **Do not** award the mark if additional names are circled unless it is clear that the correct names are the final answer.
7	10p	2	Award **TWO** marks for the correct answer of 10(p). If the answer is incorrect or missing, award **ONE** mark for a complete, correct method, e.g. • 100 − 45 − 45 = (no answer) • 100 − 2 × 45 = (no answer) • 100 − 90 = (no answer) • 100 − 45 = 65 ⇨ 65 − 45 = 15 (incorrect) • 45 × 2 = 80 ⇨ 100 − 80 = 20 (incorrect) **OR** Any of these partial methods carried out correctly but missing the correct answer, e.g. • 45 + 45 = 90 • 45 × 2 = 90 • 100 − 45 = 55
8	15	1	
Test 8			
1	✓ ✓	1	Both correct shapes must be indicated. Accept any other clear way of indicating the two correct shapes. **Do not** award the mark if additional shapes are ticked, unless it is clear that the two correct shapes are the final answer.

Answers

2		1	All three plant trays must be correctly matched. **Do not** award the mark if a plant tray is matched to more than one calculation. Ignore any extra lines drawn from the first plant tray.
3		1	All three clocks must be correctly matched. **Do not** award the mark if a clock face is matched to more than one time.
4	1 + 6 + 7 = 14	1	All four numbers in the number sentence must be correct and in the order shown.
5		1	Accept any other clear way of indicating the correct answer, e.g. circling. **Do not** award the mark if additional objects are ticked, unless it is clear that the correct object is the final answer.
6	8	1	
7	**29** + **11** = 40	1	Both numbers in the calculation must be correct.
8	10g	2	Award **TWO** marks for the correct answer of 10(g). If the answer is incorrect or missing, award **ONE** mark for a complete, correct method, e.g. • 100 − 52 − 38 = (no answer) • 52 + 38 = 80 ⇨ 100 − 80 = 20 (incorrect) **OR** Any of these partial methods carried out correctly but missing the correct answer, e.g. • 100 − 52 = 48 • 100 − 38 = 62

Reading

Question	Answer	Marks	Additional Guidance
Test 1			
1	**Award 1 mark for:** Lena	1	

101

Answers

2	**Award 1 mark for** an answer which acknowledges that she did not like sun cream/did not want the sun cream on.	1	**Do not accept** 'it felt horrible and sticky' without further explanation.
3	**Award 1 mark for:** at the beach ✓	1	
4	**Award 1 mark for** an answer which acknowledges that it was to prevent Lena getting burned.	1	**Do not accept** 'because it was hot' or 'because it was sunny'.
5	**Award 1 mark for:** glorious	1	**Also accept:** hot

Test 2

1	**Award 1 mark for both:** They are quite easy to train. ✓ Most like to be around children. ✓	1	
2	**Award 1 mark for:** Some need lots of exercise. **OR** Some need lots of space (to run around). **OR** Some are fine in smaller homes.	1	
3	**Award 1 mark for all correctly matched:** Is your house big enough? — cost of keeping a dog Your dog will need feeding. — time to look after a dog It will want to play. — size of the dog	1	
4	**Award 1 mark for** an answer which acknowledges that dogs need exercise.	1	**Accept** any answer that suggests walks are needed to keep the dog fit/healthy.
5	**Award 1 mark for** an answer which acknowledges that the question is asked in order to make you think whether you would like to take a dog out in bad weather **AND/OR** that it is designed to make you think whether you really would like to own a dog.	1	

Test 3

1	**Award 1 mark for:** he had been too afraid	1	
2	**Award 1 mark for** an answer which acknowledges that he wanted to find out the/a secret.	1	
3	**Award 1 mark for both:** It was shallow. ✓ It was muddy. ✓	1	
4	**Award 1 mark for** two or more correct answers: He had heard that a giant toad lived in the lake. *True.* It was five years since Zed had been to the lake. *False* Zed carried a backpack. *True*	1	
5	**Award 1 mark for** an answer which acknowledges that he was waiting for the giant toad/strange creature.	1	

Test 4

1	**Award 1 mark for:** a few days ✓	1	
2	**Award 1 mark for:** so you can play out for longer/play longer (in the snow).	1	

Answers

3	**Award 1 mark for:** hat ✓	1	
4	**Award 1 mark for both:** Make sure there is nothing to crash into! You must never aim for the head.	1	**Also accept:** Start on a gentle slope.
5	**Award 1 mark for:** The snow might stop them from going shopping. ✓	1	

Test 5

1	**Award 1 mark for:** fantastic	1	
2	**Award 1 mark for** two or three correct answers. **Award 2 marks for** four correct answers: Jasmin and her big brother went to a museum. *True* They looked at old bikes and cars. *True* The old lady got on the bus. *False* Jasmin's brother bought lunch from the shop. *False*	Up to 2	
3	**Award 1 mark for** 2, 3 and 4 in the correct order: Jasmin slowly got off the bus. *4* Jasmin called her teddy Blue. *1* An old lady picked up Blue. *3* They looked at model dinosaurs. *2*	1	
4	**Award 1 mark for:** Her heart sank. ✓	1	
5	**Award 1 mark for** an answer which suggests that Jasmin will get Blue back/the old lady gives Blue to Jasmin.	1	**Also accept** an answer which suggests that the old lady doesn't quite catch up with them and Jasmin does not get Blue back.

Test 6

1	**Award 1 mark for:** improve	1	
2	**Award 1 mark for:** a wetsuit ✓	1	
3	**Award 1 mark for any two of the following:** swimming pool; lake; river; sea	1	**Do not accept** reference to other water (e.g. canal, reservoir) as these are not mentioned in the text.
4	**Award 1 mark for** an answer that acknowledges that the information is about safety/keeping safe.	1	
5	**Award 1 mark for** each reason given (up to a maximum of two): • It is the easiest (to learn/to get access to). • It is the activity that people are most familiar with/are most likely to know/have already tried. • You should be able to swim before you try other watersports. • You can do it at the swimming pool/it is more accessible/ easier to find somewhere to swim.	Up to 2	

Answers

Test 7			
1	**Award 1 mark for both:** Sad Happy	1	
2	**Award 1 mark for:** in your mind ✓	1	
3	**Award 1 mark for all correctly matched:** starting sketch —— your imagination guide —— your mood brush —— your thoughts (starting sketch → your thoughts, brush → your imagination)	1	
4	**Award 1 mark for:** your special place	1	**Also accept:** '(Into) your picture, your special place'.
5	**Award 2 marks** for an answer which acknowledges: The phrases show that the ideas can be as strange as you want them to be **AND** It is down to your own imagination. **Award 1 mark** for an answer which gives just one of the points above.	Up to 2	
Test 8			
1	**Award 1 mark for:** cheese rolling ✓	1	
2	**Award 1 mark for:** hundreds of years ago	1	**Do not accept:** a long time ago
3	**Award 1 mark for:** Double Gloucester	1	
4	**Award 1 mark for** an answer which acknowledges that the cheese needs to be round so it can roll.	1	
5	**Award 2 marks for** an answer which acknowledges that: People tumble/fall down the hill/get injured Because the slope is steep/the event is fast. **Award 1 mark for** an answer which only mentions one of the points above.	Up to 2	

Grammar and Punctuation

Question	Answer	Marks	Additional Guidance
Test 1			
1	**Award 1 mark for:** because ✓	1	
2	**Award 1 mark for:** (elephant)	1	Accept other clear indication of 'elephant', e.g. ticked, underlined.
3	**Award 1 mark for** all three correct: When will the show start? Make sure you eat your lunch. Was it a long journey?	1	

4	**Award 1 mark for:** a verb ✓	1	
5	**Award 1 mark for:** (amazing)	1	Accept other clear indication of 'amazing', e.g. ticked, underlined.
6	**Award 1 mark for:** The dogs are making a loud noise. ✓	1	
7	**Award 1 mark for** a comma between the words *bread* and *cheese*: We need to buy bread, cheese and cake.	1	
8	**Award 1 mark for:** if **OR** because **OR** when **OR** as **OR** since **OR** whenever	1	
9	**Award 2 marks for** a grammatically correct sentence with the correct punctuation, e.g. • There are cows in the field. • There are trees in the field. • There are cows and trees in the field. • The cows are behind the fence. **Award 1 mark** for a grammatically correct sentence but with punctuation (e.g. the full stop, or capital letter at the beginning) missing.	Up to 2	
Test 2			
1	**Award 1 mark for:** a noun ✓	1	
2	**Award 1 mark for:** (danced)	1	Accept other clear indication of 'danced', e.g. ticked, underlined.
3	**Award 1 mark for:** Jade walks home every Friday. ✓	1	
4	**Award 1 mark for** all three correct: Where is the train station? The train will be here soon. When I get on the train, I will read.	1	
5	**Award 1 mark for:** an exclamation ✓	1	
6	**Award 1 mark for** the letters u n added to make the word *unwelcome*.	1	
7	**Award 1 mark for:** (had)	1	Accept other clear indication of 'had', e.g. ticked, underlined.
8	**Award 1 mark for** each part correct: Last week, Ethan **played** football. Today, Katie is **playing** football.	Up to 2	Also accept *Last week, Ethan **was playing** football.*
9	**Award 2 marks for** a grammatically correct and correctly punctuated command, e.g. • Tidy your bedroom now. • You must tidy up. **Award 1 mark** for a grammatically correct command but with punctuation (e.g. full stop, or capital letter at the beginning) missing.	Up to 2	Accept exclamation marks instead of full stops as final punctuation marks.

Answers

Test 3			
1	**Award 1 mark for:** an adverb ✓	1	
2	**Award 1 mark for:** (if)	1	Accept other clear indication of 'if', e.g. ticked, underlined.
3	**Award 1 mark for** all three correct: slow – adjective quickly – adverb carefully – adverb	1	
4	**Award 1 mark for:** a small sandwich ✓	1	
5	**Award 1 mark for** full stops after *sweets* and *them*: Anna had lots of sweets. Seb asked her to share them.	1	
6	**Award 1 mark for:** Leah had lunch at school. ✓	1	
7	**Award 1 mark for:** picture ✓ **AND** wall ✓	1	
8	**Award 1 mark for:** What a brilliant picture you have painted! ✓	1	
9	**Award 2 marks for** a grammatically correct sentence with the correct punctuation, e.g. • The house is big. • The house has a nice door. • I can see a big house. **Award 1 mark** for a grammatically correct sentence but with punctuation (e.g. the full stop, or capital letter at the beginning) missing.	Up to 2	
Test 4			
1	**Award 1 mark for:** but ✓	1	
2	**Award 1 mark for** a clear addition of *ly* to the end of *quick* to make *quickly*: The cat was running quickly to escape the rain.	1	
3	**Award 1 mark for:** The children are doing some maths. ✓	1	
4	**Award 1 mark for:** What kind of books do you read ✓	1	
5	**Award 1 mark for:** (and)	1	Accept other clear indication of 'and', e.g. ticked, underlined.
6	**Award 1 mark for:** a comma ✓	1	
7	**Award 1 mark for** an apostrophe between the final *m* and the *s* in *mum's*: Here is mum's new car.	1	
8	**Award 1 mark for:** unhealthy	1	Accept an incorrect spelling if the prefix 'un' is correct.

Answers

9	**Award 2 marks** for a grammatically correct sentence containing an appropriate verb, and with the correct punctuation, e.g. • The girl is running. • She was jogging. • There is a girl going for a run. **Award 1 mark** for a grammatically correct sentence containing an appropriate verb, but with punctuation (e.g. the full stop, or capital letter at the beginning) missing.	Up to 2	Do **not** accept an answer that does not include a verb.

Test 5

1	**Award 1 mark for:** an adjective ✓	1	
2	**Award 1 mark for both:** cleaned **AND** checked	1	Accept other clear indication of 'cleaned' and 'checked', e.g. ticked, underlined.
3	**Award 1 mark for:** We run, jump and skip as fast as we can. ✓	1	
4	**Award 1 mark for:** I went on holiday to Spain. *Past* Pavel is hiding under the stairs. *Present* Erin drew a picture of a rocket. *Past*	1	
5	**Award 1 mark for:** rabbits	1	Accept other clear indication of 'rabbits', e.g. ticked, underlined.
6	**Award 1 mark for:** a full stop ✓	1	
7	**Award 1 mark for:** luca's cousin is from italy. ✓ (Luca and Italy should begin with a capital letter.)	1	
8	**Award 2 marks** for a grammatically correct statement with the correct punctuation, i.e. The garden is big. **Award 1 mark** for the correct statement but with punctuation (e.g. the full stop, or capital letter at the beginning) missing.	Up to 2	
9	**Award 2 marks** for a grammatically correct question with the correct punctuation, e.g. • What time is it? • Do you have the time please? **Award 1 mark** for a grammatically correct question but with punctuation (e.g. the full stop, or capital letter at the beginning) missing.	Up to 2	

Test 6

1	**Award 1 mark for:** a command ✓	1	
2	**Award 1 mark for:** and	1	Accept other clear indication of 'and', e.g. ticked, underlined.
3	**Award 1 mark for both:** Carefully ✓ **AND** quietly ✓	1	
4	**Award 1 mark for:** a comma ✓ (A comma is needed between the words When and where.)	1	

Answers

5	**Award 1 mark for both:** (picked) **AND** (placed)	1	Accept other clear indication of 'picked' and 'placed', e.g. ticked, underlined.
6	**Award 1 mark for:** (although)	1	Accept other clear indication of 'although', e.g. ticked, underlined.
7	**Award 1 mark for:** wouldn't	1	
8	**Award 1 mark for:** ate	1	
9	**Award 1 mark for** each part correct: • Yesterday, I **baked/made/cooked/held** a cake. • Today, I am **baking/making/cooking/creating** a cake.	Up to 2	

Test 7

1	**Award 1 mark for:** an adjective ✓	1	
2	**Award 1 mark for:** (and)	1	Accept other clear indication of 'and', e.g. ticked, underlined.
3	**Award 1 mark for:** sad – ness (sadness) entertain – ment (entertainment) kind – ness (kindness)	1	
4	**Award 1 mark for:** Dan will make dinner. ✓	1	
5	**Award 1 mark for both:** (yesterday) **AND** (emma)	1	Accept other clear indication of 'yesterday' and 'emma', e.g. ticked, underlined.
6	**Award 1 mark for:** They'll ✓	1	
7	**Award 1 mark for:** mice *Plural* animals *Plural* person *Singular*	1	
8	**Award 1 mark for** an acknowledgement that Spain is a proper noun, e.g. • It is the name of a place. • It is a name. • It is a proper noun.	1	Do **not** accept: *Because it is a noun.*
9	**Award 2 marks** for a grammatically correct sentence with the correct punctuation, e.g. • There are rides at the fair. • There is a carousel and a big wheel. **Award 1 mark** for a grammatically correct sentence but with punctuation (e.g. the full stop, or capital letter at the beginning) missing.	Up to 2	

Test 8

1	**Award 1 mark for:** unhelpful ✓	1	
2	**Award 1 mark for:** (practises)	1	Accept other clear indication of 'practises', e.g. ticked, underlined.

Answers

3	**Award 1 mark for:** an adjective ✓	1	
4	**Award 1 mark for:** They are eating their favourite food. *Present* Annie is playing the piano. *Present* We have made a wooden doll. *Past*	1	
5	**Award 1 mark** for a question mark between the words *home* and *Ali*: When would they get home? Ali was feeling tired.	1	
6	**Award 1 mark for:** a capital letter ✓ (The first word in a sentence should start with a capital letter.)	1	
7	**Award 1 mark for:** (so)	1	Accept other clear indication of 'so', e.g. ticked, underlined.
8	**Award 1 mark for:** help ✓ **AND** use ✓	1	
9	**Award 2 marks** for a grammatically correct exclamation with the correct punctuation, e.g. • What a great picture you have drawn! • What an amazing picture I can see! **Award 1 mark** for a grammatically correct exclamation but with punctuation (e.g. the full stop, or capital letter at the beginning) missing.	Up to 2	

Spelling

Transcripts and answers

Before each spelling test, read this instruction to your child:
I am going to read ten sentences to you. Each sentence has a word missing. Listen carefully to the missing word and write this in the answer space, making sure that you spell it correctly. I will read the word, then the word within a sentence, then I will repeat the word a third time.
You should now read the spellings three times, as given below. Leave at least a 12-second gap between spellings. At the end, read all the sentences again, giving your child the chance to make any changes they wish to their answers.
Award **1 mark** for each correct spelling.

Test 1			Test (continued)	
1	*The word is **hutch**.* The rabbit lives in a **hutch**. *The word is **hutch**.*		7	*The word is **badly**.* He was not hurt **badly** when he fell. *The word is **badly**.*
2	*The word is **jumped**.* We **jumped** into the swimming pool. *The word is **jumped**.*		8	*The word is **funny**.* We watched a **funny** show at the circus. *The word is **funny**.*
3	*The word is **kit**.* I changed into my PE **kit**. *The word is **kit**.*		9	*The word is **bedroom**.* Olivia will soon have a new **bedroom**. *The word is **bedroom**.*
4	*The word is **near**.* The house was **near** the shops. *The word is **near**.*		10	*The word is **bottle**.* The **bottle** smashed on the floor. *The word is **bottle**.*
5	*The word is **some**.* There are **some** cakes at Gran's house. *The word is **some**.*		**Test 2**	
			1	*The word is **right**.* Turn **right** at the next junction. *The word is **right**.*
6	*The word is **metal**.* Her new watch has a **metal** strap. *The word is **metal**.*		2	*The word is **city**.* London is a large **city**. *The word is **city**.*

3	*The word is* **said**. Sara **said** she could not play today. *The word is* **said**.
4	*The word is* **tunnel**. The train went through a long **tunnel**. *The word is* **tunnel**.
5	*The word is* **easiest**. It was the **easiest** dance they had ever seen. *The word is* **easiest**.
6	*The word is* **wash**. The children had to **wash** the car. *The word is* **wash**.
7	*The word is* **other**. My friend was on the **other** side of the road. *The word is* **other**.
8	*The word is* **turn**. Freya took her **turn** to throw the ball. *The word is* **turn**.
9	*The word is* **knee**. Mum hurt her **knee** playing netball. *The word is* **knee**.
10	*The word is* **dry**. They used a towel to **dry** themselves. *The word is* **dry**.

Test 3

1	*The word is* **write**. The class had to **write** a story. *The word is* **write**.
2	*The word is* **animal**. Kenji's favourite **animal** is the giraffe. *The word is* **animal**.
3	*The word is* **bathroom**. Somebody left the tap running in the **bathroom**. *The word is* **bathroom**.
4	*The word is* **dream**. Jess had a very strange **dream**. *The word is* **dream**.
5	*The word is* **think**. We **think** we will visit the museum tomorrow. *The word is* **think**.
6	*The word is* **give**. Each week, they **give** to charity. *The word is* **give**.
7	*The word is* **watch**. For his birthday, Owen got a **watch**. *The word is* **watch**.
8	*The word is* **station**. The train was late leaving the **station**. *The word is* **station**.
9	*The word is* **friend**. Amy waited for her **friend**. *The word is* **friend**.

10	*The word is* **bike**. Liam had a new **bike**. *The word is* **bike**.

Test 4

1	*The word is* **off**. Dad wiped the dirt **off** his shoes. *The word is* **off**.
2	*The word is* **garden**. The children played in the **garden**. *The word is* **garden**.
3	*The word is* **travel**. Mum has to **travel** far to work. *The word is* **travel**.
4	*The word is* **chimney**. Smoke was coming from the **chimney**. *The word is* **chimney**.
5	*The word is* **section**. A **section** of the roof was leaking. *The word is* **section**.
6	*The word is* **sound**. He could hear the **sound** of his own breathing. *The word is* **sound**.
7	*The word is* **usual**. They went to their **usual** holiday destination. *The word is* **usual**.
8	*The word is* **should**. Mum decided that we **should** leave soon. *The word is* **should**.
9	*The word is* **always**. I **always** brush my teeth at bedtime. *The word is* **always**.
10	*The word is* **dolphin**. It was amazing to see a **dolphin** in the harbour. *The word is* **dolphin**.

Test 5

1	*The word is* **working**. The children were **working** in the library. *The word is* **working**.
2	*The word is* **pitch**. All of the players walked onto the **pitch**. *The word is* **pitch**.
3	*The word is* **wood**. The benches were all made of **wood**. *The word is* **wood**.
4	*The word is* **cage**. The rescued tiger was put in a **cage**. *The word is* **cage**.
5	*The word is* **again**. We went to see the film **again**. *The word is* **again**.
6	*The word is* **danced**. Everybody **danced** at the school disco. *The word is* **danced**.

Answers

7	*The word is* **mouth**. Stevie put the bread in his **mouth**. *The word is* **mouth**.
8	*The word is* **squash**. The children had a drink of orange **squash**. *The word is* **squash**.
9	*The word is* **sadness**. There was great **sadness** when the teacher retired. *The word is* **sadness**.
10	*The word is* **knock**. Mo heard the **knock** at the door. *The word is* **knock**.

Test 6

1	*The word is* **back**. The geese all flew **back** home. *The word is* **back**.
2	*The word is* **warm**. It was **warm** in the cinema. *The word is* **warm**.
3	*The word is* **race**. The **race** was very fast. *The word is* **race**.
4	*The word is* **under**. **Under** the bed is a box of secrets. *The word is* **under**.
5	*The word is* **complete**. It took ages to **complete** the journey. *The word is* **complete**.
6	*The word is* **cooked**. Mrs Smith **cooked** a meal. *The word is* **cooked**.
7	*The word is* **television**. The **television** was on all day. *The word is* **television**.
8	*The word is* **small**. **Small** insects covered the plants. *The word is* **small**.
9	*The word is* **lace**. Jane helped me tie my **lace**. *The word is* **lace**.
10	*The word is* **wrong**. He knew it was **wrong** so he said sorry. *The word is* **wrong**.

Test 7

1	*The word is* **happy**. The class assembly made everyone **happy**. *The word is* **happy**.
2	*The word is* **wheel**. The go-kart lost a **wheel** on the hill. *The word is* **wheel**.
3	*The word is* **well**. We all did **well** in the tests. *The word is* **well**.

4	*The word is* **cave**. The paintings were found in a hidden **cave**. *The word is* **cave**.
5	*The word is* **seat**. I could not find my **seat** at the football match. *The word is* **seat**.
6	*The word is* **quickest**. Harry found the **quickest** way to the lake. *The word is* **quickest**.
7	*The word is* **word**. I got only one **word** wrong in my spellings. *The word is* **word**.
8	*The word is* **treasure**. It is believed that the **treasure** was hidden nearby. *The word is* **treasure**.
9	*The word is* **local**. They only went shopping in **local** shops. *The word is* **local**.
10	*The word is* **easier**. It is **easier** to walk to school sometimes. *The word is* **easier**.

Test 8

1	*The word is* **bear**. Her best photograph was of a **bear**. *The word is* **bear**.
2	*The word is* **skin**. Millie had a rash on her **skin**. *The word is* **skin**.
3	*The word is* **where**. I did not know **where** the car was parked. *The word is* **where**.
4	*The word is* **rocks**. There were many hiding places in the **rocks**. *The word is* **rocks**.
5	*The word is* **bank**. They went to the **bank** to get some money. *The word is* **bank**.
6	*The word is* **swan**. The ugly duckling turned into a beautiful **swan**. *The word is* **swan**.
7	*The word is* **nothing**. There was **nothing** they could do to help. *The word is* **nothing**.
8	*The word is* **runner**. Lou was the fastest **runner** in the school. *The word is* **runner**.
9	*The word is* **tried**. The whole team **tried** really hard. *The word is* **tried**.
10	*The word is* **football**. We found a **football** in the duck pond. *The word is* **football**.

Score Chart

You have completed all the tests! Now write your scores in the score chart below.

Test	Arithmetic	Reasoning	Reading	Grammar and punctuation	Spelling
Test 1	/12	/8	/5	/10	/10
Test 2	/12	/9	/5	/11	/10
Test 3	/12	/9	/5	/10	/10
Test 4	/12	/9	/5	/10	/10
Test 5	/12	/9	/6	/11	/10
Test 6	/12	/9	/6	/10	/10
Test 7	/12	/9	/6	/10	/10
Test 8	/12	/9	/6	/10	/10
TOTAL	/96	/71	/44	/82	/80

How did you do?

I did brilliantly!
Fabulous!

I did well.
Great stuff!

I did ok.
Well done – keep up the practice if you want to improve.

I didn't do so well.
Don't worry – there's still time to learn and practise. Why not try these tests again?